Left-Handed Childı
Guitar Chord Book

by William Bay

Table of Contents

How to Read Chord Diagrams 2	E Chord 17
EZ C Chord 3	Building the F Chord 18
EZ G7 Chord 4	F Chord/4 Strings 19
EZ G Chord 5	C7 Chord 20
D7 Chord 6	B♭ Chord 21
D Chord 7	Key of C Chord Progression 22
A7 Chord 8	B minor Chord 22
A minor Chord 9	Key of G Chord Progression 22
D minor Chord 10	F♯ minor Chord (F♯m) 23
E7 Chord 11	C♯ minor Chord (C♯m) 23
A Chord 12	G♯ minor Chord (G♯m) 24
Full C Chord 13	G minor Chord 24
Full G7 Chord 14	Rock Power Chords 25
Full G Chord 14	Blues Progressions 28
E minor Chord 15	Chord Diagrams 30
B7 Chord 16	Capo Chart 32

1   2

Visit us on the Web at www.melbay.com — E-mail us at email@melbay.com

How to Read Chord Diagrams

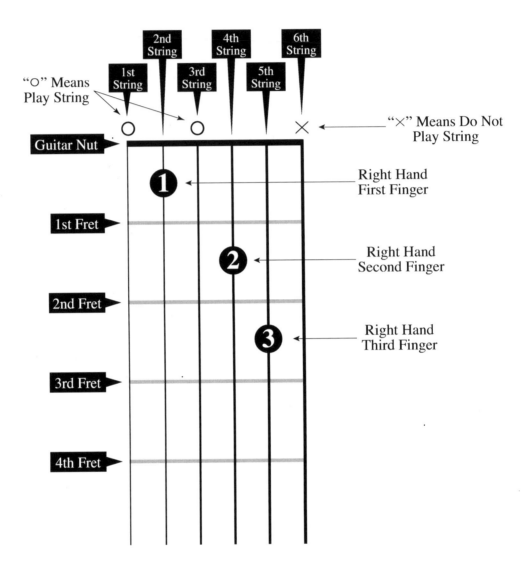

- Vertical lines are strings
- Horizontal lines are frets
- Circled numbers are right-handed fingers
- Small "o" over a string means to play the string open (no fingers pressing down)
- "×" over a string means not to play that string

EZ C Chord
Play only top 3 strings

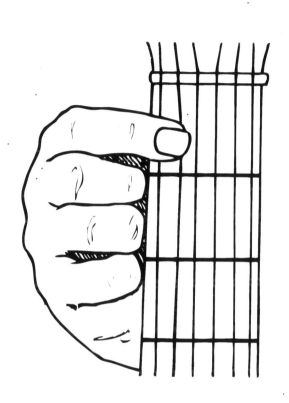
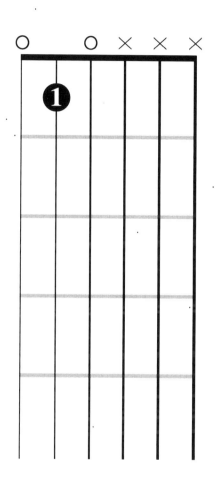

EZ G7 Chord
Play only top 4 strings

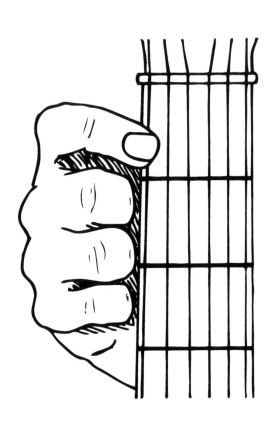

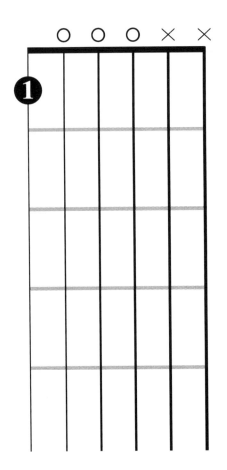

Strum mark (╱) means to strum the chord. Strum Down from the lowest or fattest strings to the highest or thin strings.

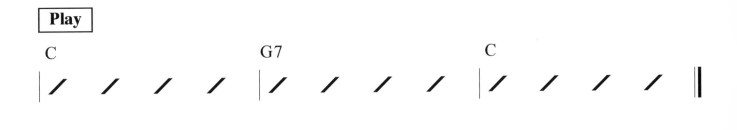

EZ G Chord
Play only top 4 strings

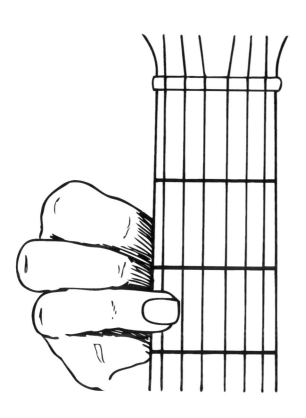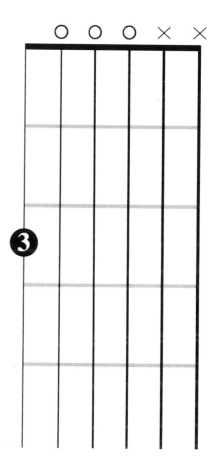

Play

C   G   G7   C

D7 Chord
Play only top 4 strings

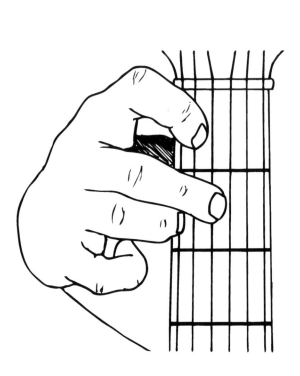

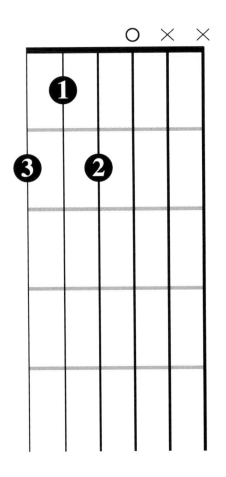

Play

D Chord
Play only top 4 strings

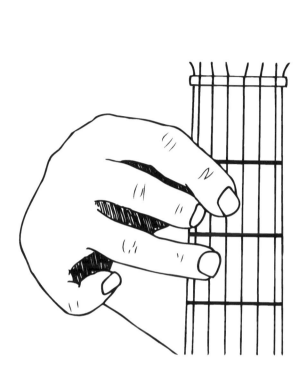

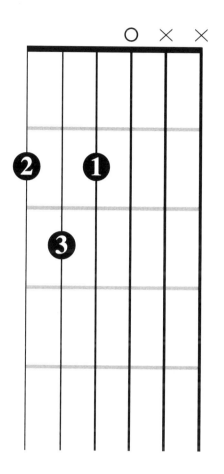

Play

C   D   D7   G   G7   C

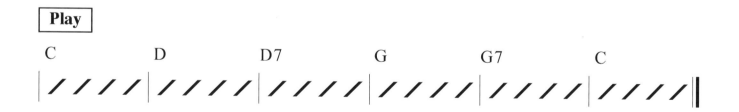

A7 Chord
Play only top 5 strings

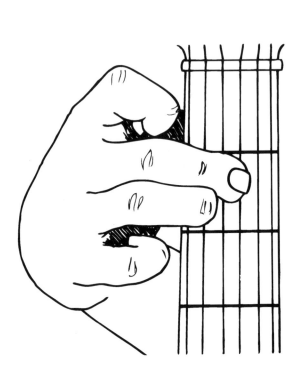

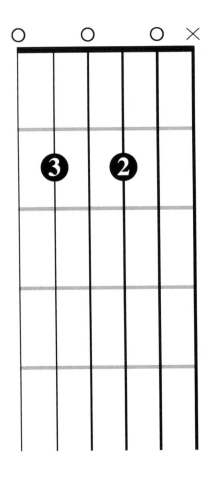

Play

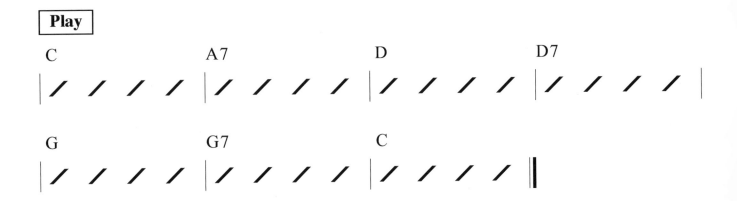

A minor Chord
(Am)

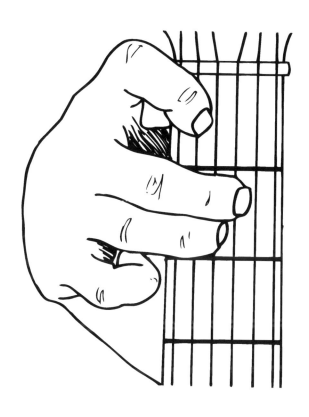 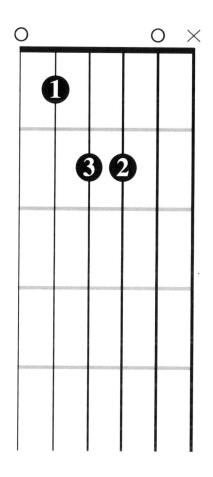

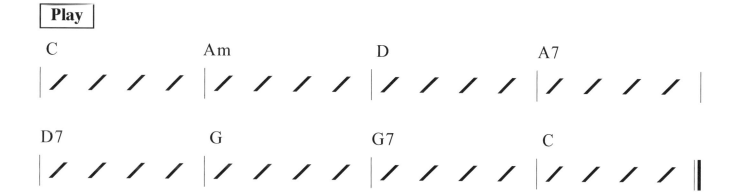

Play

| C | Am | D | A7 |
| D7 | G | G7 | C |

D minor Chord
(Dm)

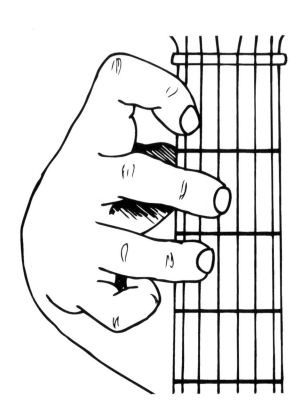

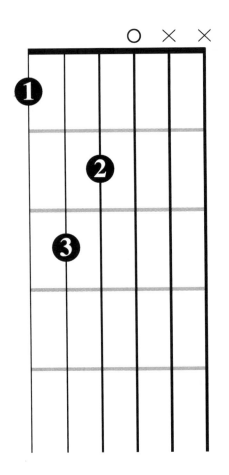

Play

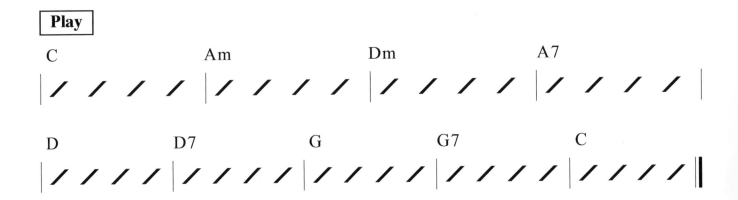

C   Am   Dm   A7

D   D7   G   G7   C

E7 Chord
Play all 6 strings

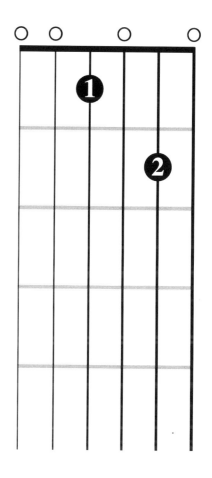

Play

C	E7	Am	Dm	A7
/ / / /	/ / / /	/ / / /	/ / / /	/ / / /

D	D7	G	G7	C
/ / / /	/ / / /	/ / / /	/ / / /	/ / / /

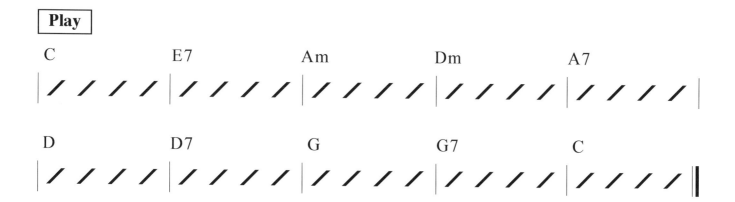

A Chord

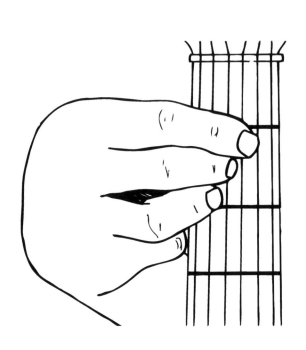 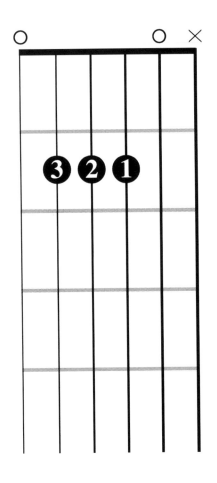

Play

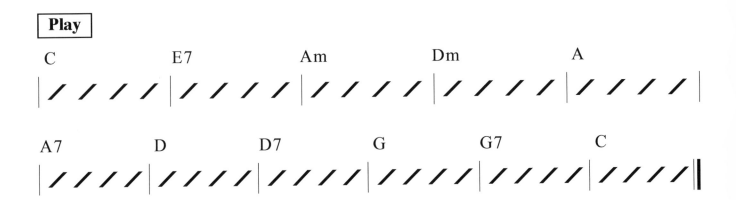

Full C Chord

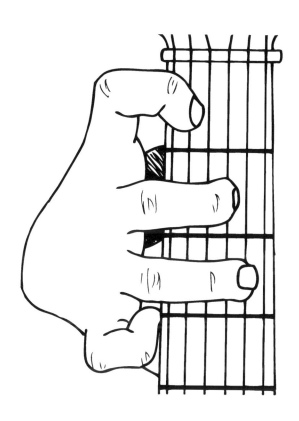 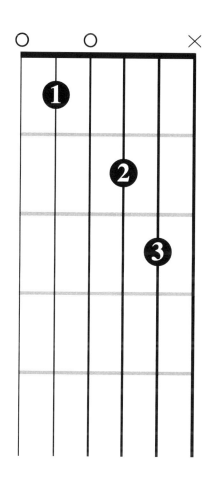

Play using the Full C Chord

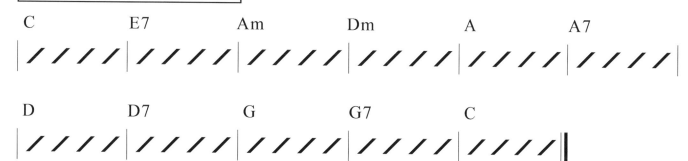

C   E7   Am   Dm   A   A7

D   D7   G   G7   C

Full G7 Chord

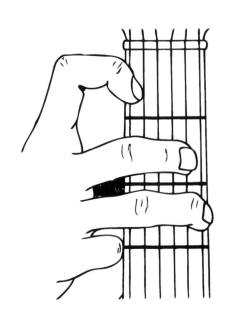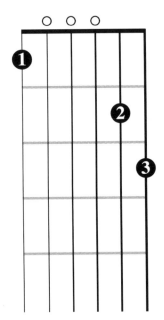

Full G Chord

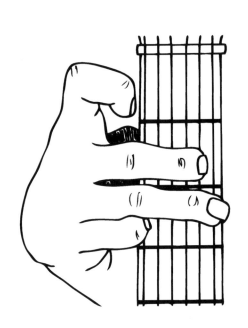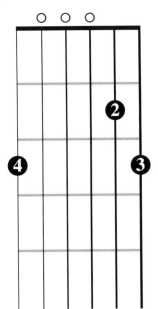

Play using the Full C, G and G7 Chords

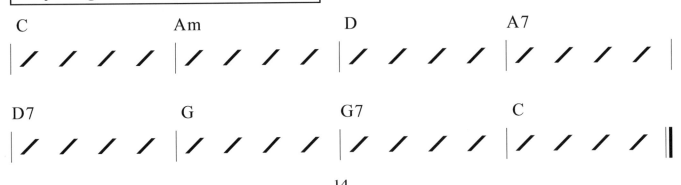

| C | Am | D | A7 |
| / / / / | / / / / | / / / / | / / / / |

| D7 | G | G7 | C |
| / / / / | / / / / | / / / / | / / / / |

E minor Chord
(Em)

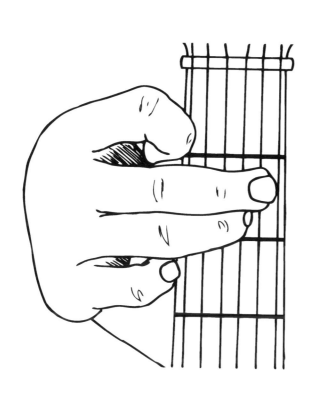

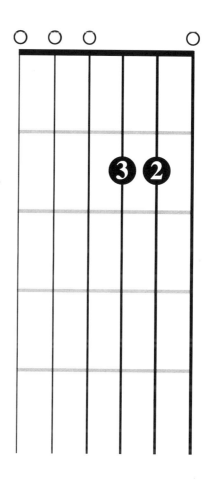

Play

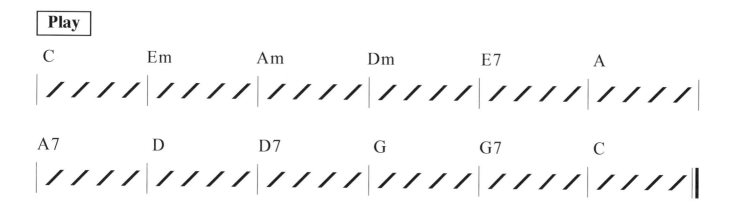

B7 Chord

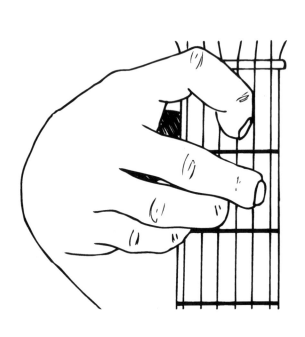 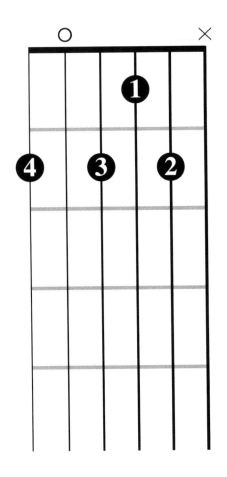

Play

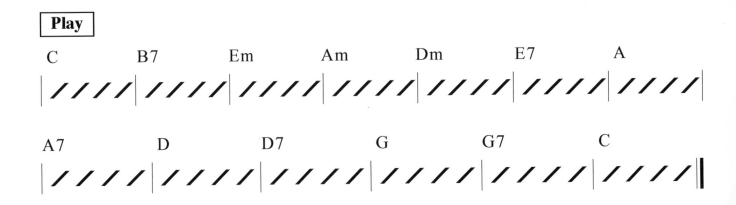

C   B7   Em   Am   Dm   E7   A

A7   D   D7   G   G7   C

E Chord

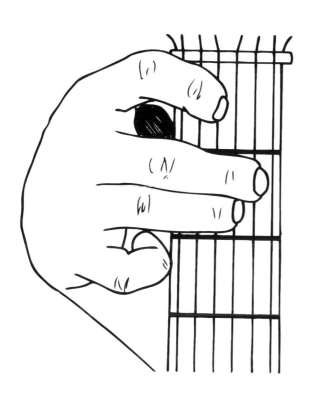 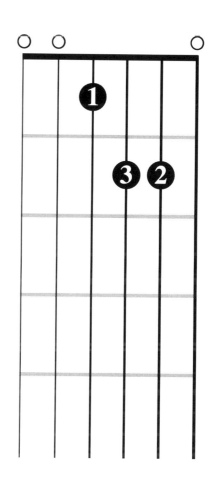

Play

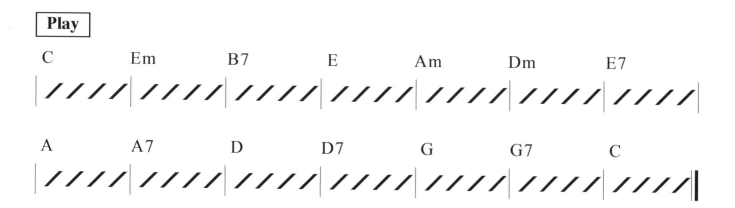

C   Em   B7   E   Am   Dm   E7

A   A7   D   D7   G   G7   C

Building the F Chord
Play only the top two strings – F/2 note chord

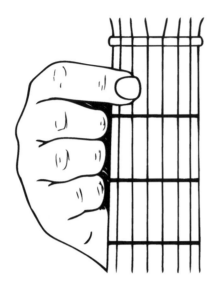 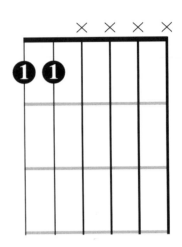

Play the following study moving up the frets – 1 fret at a time

F	1st fret	2nd fret	3rd fret	4th fret	5th fret

‖ ╱ ╱ ╱ ╱ | ╱ ╱ ╱ ╱ | ╱ ╱ ╱ ╱ | ╱ ╱ ╱ ╱ | ╱ ╱ ╱ ╱ ‖

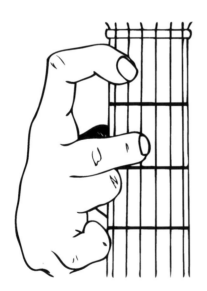 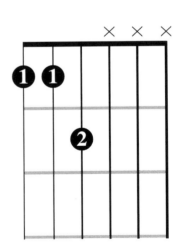

Play the following study using the F chords / 3-note form moving up 1 fret at a time

F	1st fret	2nd fret	3rd fret	4th fret	5th fret

‖ ╱ ╱ ╱ ╱ | ╱ ╱ ╱ ╱ | ╱ ╱ ╱ ╱ | ╱ ╱ ╱ ╱ | ╱ ╱ ╱ ╱ ‖

F Chord / 4 Strings

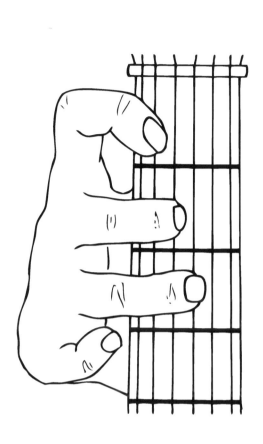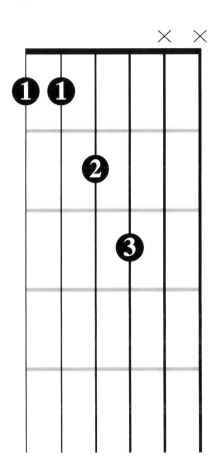

Play the following study using the F chord / 4-string form – moving up the fingerboard 1 fret at a time.

F   1st fret   2nd fret   3rd fret   4th fret   5th fret

| / / / / | / / / / | / / / / | / / / / | / / / / ‖

Play

C   F   C   Em   B7

| / / / / | / / / / | / / / / | / / / / | / / / / |

E   Am   Dm   E7   A   A7

| / / / / | / / / / | / / / / | / / / / | / / / / | / / / / |

D   D7   G   F   G7   C

| / / / / | / / / / | / / / / | / / / / | / / / / | / / / / ‖

19

C7 Chord

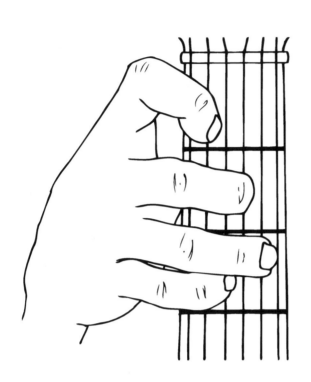 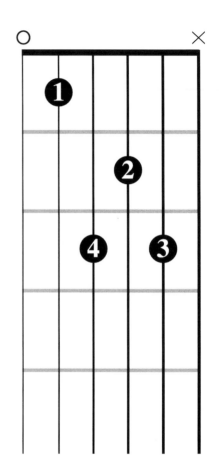

Play

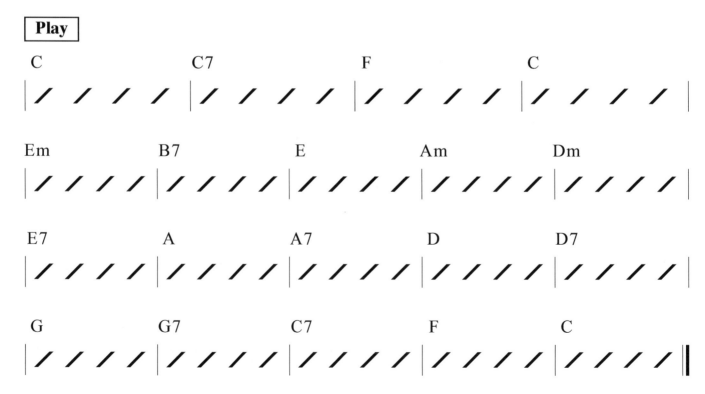

C	C7	F	C
/ / / /	/ / / /	/ / / /	/ / / /

Em	B7	E	Am	Dm
/ / / /	/ / / /	/ / / /	/ / / /	/ / / /

E7	A	A7	D	D7
/ / / /	/ / / /	/ / / /	/ / / /	/ / / /

G	G7	C7	F	C
/ / / /	/ / / /	/ / / /	/ / / /	/ / / /

Bb Chord

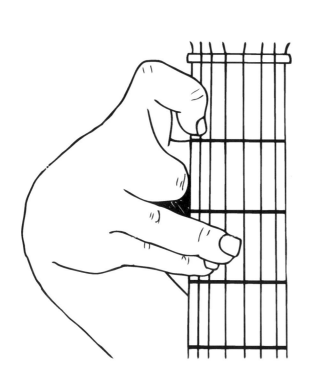 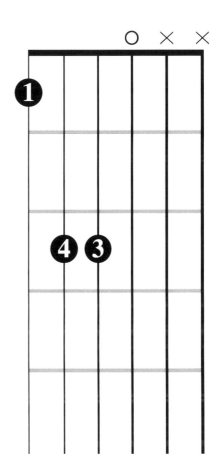

Play

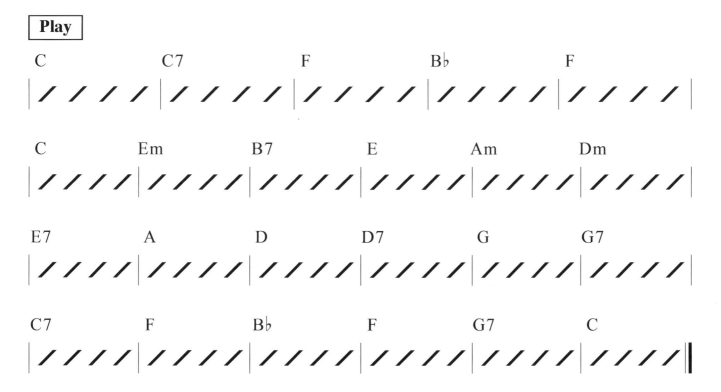

Key of C Chord Progression

Play

C	Em	Am	Dm	G7	C
/ / / /	/ / / /	/ / / /	/ / / /	/ / / /	/ / / /

B minor Chord

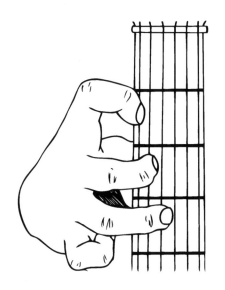 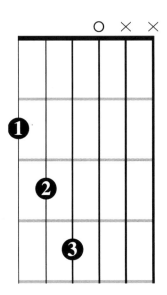

Key of G Chord Progression

Play

G	Bm	Em	Am	D7	G
/ / / /	/ / / /	/ / / /	/ / / /	/ / / /	/ / / /

F# minor Chord
(F#m)

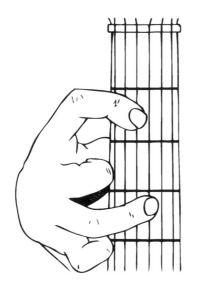

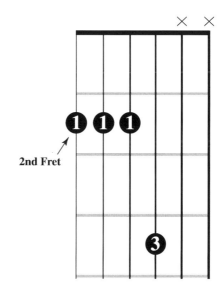

2nd Fret

Key of D Chord Progression

D	F#m	Bm	Em	A7	D
/ / / /	/ / / /	/ / / /	/ / / /	/ / / /	/ / / /

C# minor Chord
(C#m)

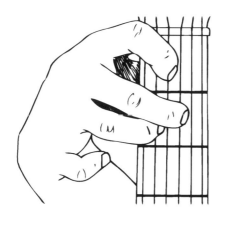

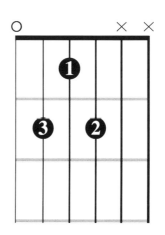

Key of A Chord Progression

A	C#m	F#m	Bm	E7	A
/ / / /	/ / / /	/ / / /	/ / / /	/ / / /	/ / / /

G♯ minor Chord
(G♯m)

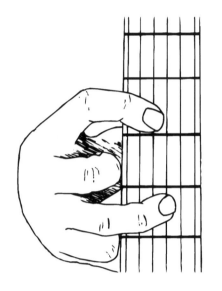 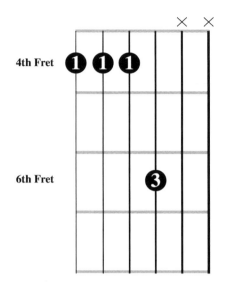

4th Fret ❶ ❶ ❶

6th Fret ❸

Key of E Chord Progression

E	G♯m	C♯m	F♯m	B7	E
/ / / /	/ / / /	/ / / /	/ / / /	/ / / /	/ / / /

G minor Chord

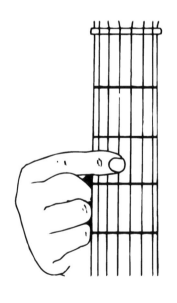 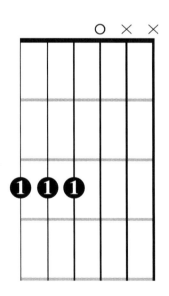

❶ ❶ ❶

Key of F Chord Progression

F	Am	Dm	Gm	C7	F
/ / / /	/ / / /	/ / / /	/ / / /	/ / / /	/ / / /

Rock Power Chords

Key of C

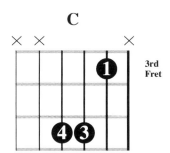
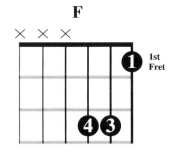
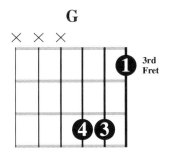

Play the following using Key of C Power Chords

C   C   F   F

| / / / / | / / / / | / / / / | / / / / |

G   G   C   C

| / / / / | / / / / | / / / / | / / / / ‖

Key of G

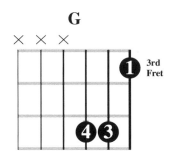
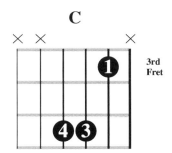
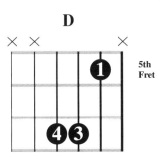

Play the following using Key of G Power Chords

G   G   C   C

| / / / / | / / / / | / / / / | / / / / |

D   D   G   G

| / / / / | / / / / | / / / / | / / / / ‖

25

Rock Power Chords

Key of D

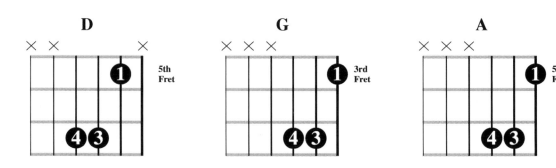

Play the following using Key of D Power Chords

| D | D | G | G |
| / / / / | / / / / | / / / / | / / / / |

| A | A | D | D |
| / / / / | / / / / | / / / / | / / / / |

Key of G

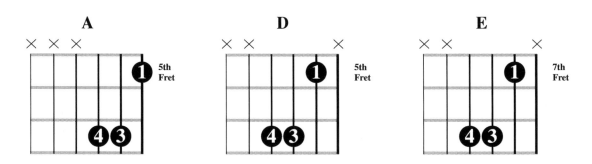

Play the following using Key of A Power Chords

| A | A | D | D |
| / / / / | / / / / | / / / / | / / / / |

| E | E | A | A |
| / / / / | / / / / | / / / / | / / / / |

Rock Power Chords

Key of E

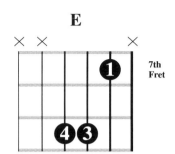

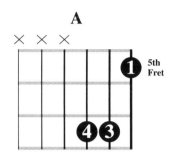

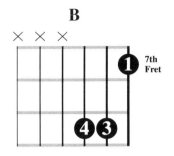

Play the following using Key of E Power Chords

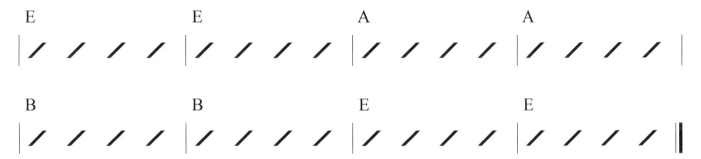

Key of F

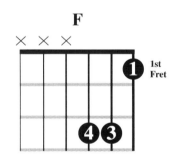

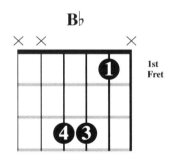

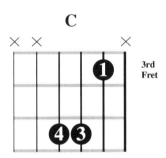

Play the following using Key of F Power Chords

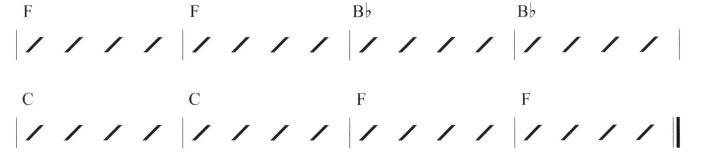

Blues Progression

Key of C

C	F	C	C7	F	F
/ / / /	/ / / /	/ / / /	/ / / /	/ / / /	/ / / /

C	C	G	F	C	C
/ / / /	/ / / /	/ / / /	/ / / /	/ / / /	/ / / /

Key of G

G	C	G	G7	C	C
/ / / /	/ / / /	/ / / /	/ / / /	/ / / /	/ / / /

G	G	D7	C7	G	G
/ / / /	/ / / /	/ / / /	/ / / /	/ / / /	/ / / /

Key of D

D	G	D	D7	G	G
/ / / /	/ / / /	/ / / /	/ / / /	/ / / /	/ / / /

D	D	A7	G7	D	D
/ / / /	/ / / /	/ / / /	/ / / /	/ / / /	/ / / /

Blues Progression

Key of A

A	D	A	A7	D	D
/ / / /	/ / / /	/ / / /	/ / / /	/ / / /	/ / / /

A	A	E7	D7	A	A
/ / / /	/ / / /	/ / / /	/ / / /	/ / / /	/ / / /

Key of E

E	A	E	E7	A	A
/ / / /	/ / / /	/ / / /	/ / / /	/ / / /	/ / / /

E	E	B7	A7	E	E
/ / / /	/ / / /	/ / / /	/ / / /	/ / / /	/ / / /

Key of F

F	B♭	F	F	B♭	B♭
/ / / /	/ / / /	/ / / /	/ / / /	/ / / /	/ / / /

F	F	C7	B♭	F	F
/ / / /	/ / / /	/ / / /	/ / / /	/ / / /	/ / / /

Major Key

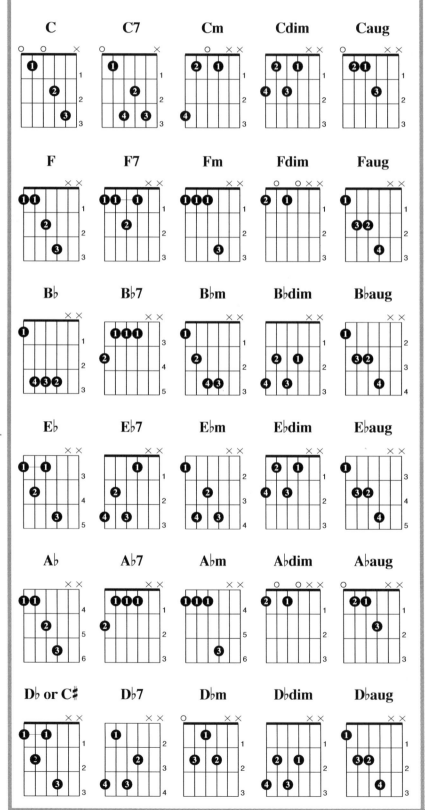

Relative Minor

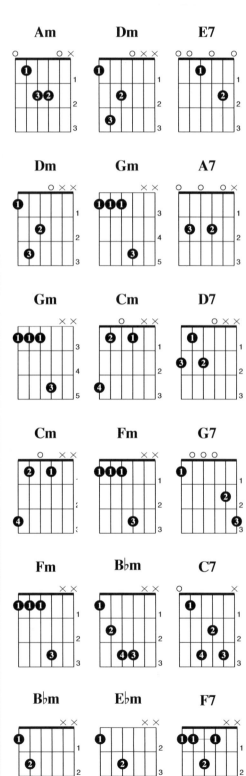

Chart

Major Key

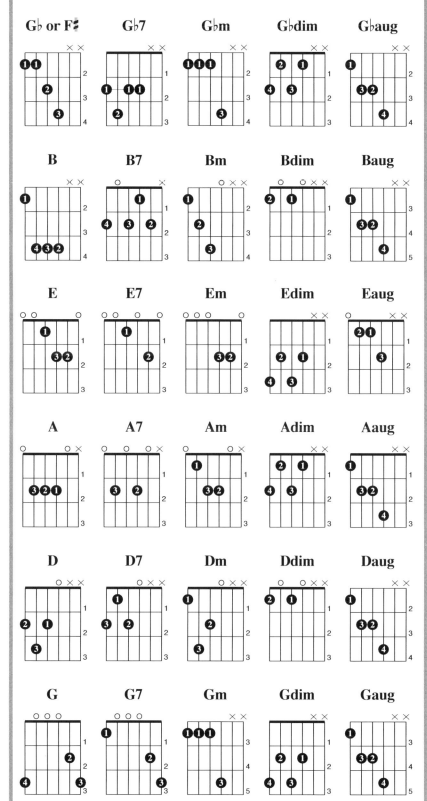

Relative Minor

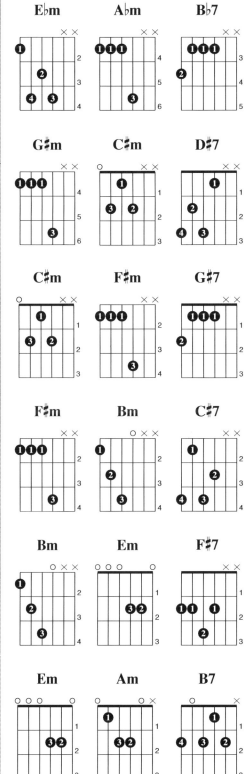

Capo Chart

Actual Sound of Chord

Capo on

Fret #	1	2	3	4	5	6	7	8	9	10	11	12
C	C# / Db	D	D# / Eb	E	F	F# / Gb	G	G# / Ab	A	A# / Bb	B	C
C# / Db	D	D# / Eb	E	F	F# / Gb	G	G# / Ab	A	A# / Bb	B	C	C# / Db
D	D# / Eb	E	F	F# / Gb	G	G# / Ab	A	A# / Bb	B	C	C# / Db	D
D# / Eb	E	F	F# / Gb	G	G# / Ab	A	A# / Bb	B	C	C# / Db	D	D# / Eb
E	F	F# / Gb	G	G# / Ab	A	A# / Bb	B	C	C# / Db	D	D# / Eb	E
F	F# / Gb	G	G# / Ab	A	A# / Bb	B	C	C# / Db	D	D# / Eb	E	F
F# / Gb	G	G# / Ab	A	A# / Bb	B	C	C# / Db	D	D# / Eb	E	F	F# / Gb
G	G# / Ab	A	A# / Bb	B	C	C# / Db	D	D# / Eb	E	F	F# / Gb	G
G# / Ab	A	A# / Bb	B	C	C# / Db	D	D# / Eb	E	F	F# / Gb	G	G# / Ab
A	A# / Bb	B	C	C# / Db	D	D# / Eb	E	F	F# / Gb	G	G# / Ab	A
A# / Bb	B	C	C# / Db	D	D# / Eb	E	F	F# / Gb	G	G# / Ab	A	A# / Bb
B	C	C# / Db	D	D# / Eb	E	F	F# / Gb	G	G# / Ab	A	A# / Bb	B

Chord held

32

Printed in Great Britain
by Amazon